Playing Bodies

Bob Perelman

Playing Bodies

Francie Shaw

Granary Books   2004   New York City

Printed and bound in Hong Kong
Cover image by Francie Shaw

                    Library of Congress Cataloging-in-Publication Data

Perelman, Bob.
    Playing bodies/ Bob Perelman, Francie Shaw.
          p. cm.
    ISBN 1-87123-64-4 (alk. paper)
    I. Shaw, Francie. II. Title.
    PS3566.E6912P58 2004
    811'.54--dc22

                                            2003025991

Granary Books, Inc.
307 Seventh Ave. Suite 1401
New York, NY 10001
www.granarybooks.com

Distributed to the trade by
D.A.P/Distributed Art Publishers   Orders: (800) 338-BOOK
155 Avenue of the Americas, Second Floor Tel. (212)627-1999
New York, NY 10013-1507   Fax (212)627-9484

Susan Stewart

A work in paintings and poetry by Francie Shaw and Bob Perelman

Not long ago I spent an afternoon visiting Francie Shaw's studio in Mt. Airy and there I saw many wonders, including a wall of small square paintings in blue and white. Each of these paintings depicted two figures—a dinosaur and a form of human being—engaged physically with one another. They were, you could say, more drafted than painted in blue on a white ground. And each acquired a certain theatrical depth from the prominent use of shadows. It was as if the flat and picturesque world of the images on Delft tiles had been transposed into some transforming combat out of Ovid, now shown under a spotlight. And although the tradition of conversation paintings seemed to be evoked, the conversation here appeared as a mysterious and silent form of mutual conversion.

Because my mind tends to read the world like a page, I started to look from left to right and top to bottom. Was evolution going backwards? Was a pre-ice-age epic unfolding? Were these strangely gendered and ungendered, anthropomorphic and animalistic, pairs engaged in agony or reunion? Was this the sexuality of pre-history or of the future? It was impossible and just plain wrong to read these paintings as a narrative, and yet each showed some moment, some tableau where a fate was being wrestled or a rescue attempted.

Francie herself has written of these images "When I started playing with the figures I was immediately intrigued with the strangeness of the size relationship. The dino is just a little bigger, but big enough to be too hard to control, small enough to grasp. That's how I feel about my thoughts and feelings—when I can grasp them even...I really see these as an inner landscape."

The Dutch sealed the interiors of their domestic space with smooth surfaces and centered images, cool tiles squarely surrounding the uncontainability of fire and the ambiguity of thresholds. But history really happens inside a house; we haunt ourselves and grapple and emerge. Mortal beings are finite, yet in play outcomes can be open-ended.

In Bob's sequence of brief lyrics, a single voice seems to speak to an absent other. Each lyric is bracketed by silence, as printed lyrics always are. These poems have the tone of someone struck in retrospection by a visual memory, someone struggling toward an understanding of whatever it is in experience that has made the very terms of understanding possible. Preoccupied with this history under the interest of another, the lyric voice produces a train of insights that are alternately ironic, erotic, saddened, and joyful.

This isn't the first collaboration between Francie Shaw and Bob Perelman, but there's something that seems about to be born in these works. They speak to the struggle of collaboration and cohabitation in the confined and enabling space of the emotions.

Playing Bodies

1   In the beginning
     I was already stuck in something
     that's me
     underneath the heavy pinch

     Day covers night, night
     breaks plastic scissors, plastic scissors
     cut Milky Way, it's
     a one-way street
     old as houses

     That's me or something
     stepping through no door
     with the light left on
     upside down, on the march

2   If you weren't
     outside the whole thing
     watching it like a hawk
     in eternity
     making snap judgments

     then maybe you could help

3

I want it
away from me
and I'll push
as hard as I have to

It's wrong
and if it doesn't go back off the wrong spot
I'll kiss it
right in the kisser

It's not right
that you're here
I need you
pushed off the right spot

4   I'd like to think my body
      knows about me more or less
      cares for what I think
      can work with my personal angles
      maybe even get a jump on them

      But whenever I find any
      scrap of dream
      it's pretty clear it's drawn a blank
      or it takes a perverse pleasure in anything but me

      I suppose I should thank our lucky stars
      that at least we're the same size
      more or less

5

I want you
more than I
have you

I want to be you
more than I
want you

6   Fuck real toy inside
pull fate in
such a soft thing
loose in the instant

Royal toy stars spinning
loose inside
a sip

Such a soft thing to pull
one inside and one around
faces gone

Let fate come
tipped in the instant
inside toy real fuck

7

Now I'm more
than those addled noises
Now I'm exactly what I say
Nothing before

Before nothing
I declare myself my boss
No far-off dice
already rolled
Nothing else

No more awful lesson
Time to unmemorize the long prayer whips skips scars
the punch the fire the hole
From now on, unmemorized

Trot along dog
the sacred record's gone

8   If I'm
     rocking back but pulling where
     you're
     leaning
     toward the point where we'll
     balance if you'll just
     hold
     me still everything will still be the
     same
     for you–agreed?

9   Meet my friend
       Contemptible Puppet

       Whatever I do
       nods silent happy approval
       Happy meal I grab
       by the middle
       shaking it open

       Watch me
       Like this

       C'mon! Yum!
       Have some!

10 This was that time
you were coming
to stay with us
on the island forever

You can see us
waving hello so happy
You can't get here soon enough

Big waves all afternoon
who cares
Once you're here
we'll be
the same size forever

We can't wait!

11   You don't have to pay
       to join the club

       The guy at the door
       will let you in free

       Just take off your code
       and let people see

       And after they touch it
       they keep the key

12   My balls were never exactly
beautiful
but before my head

was so deflated
they weren't half bad
when you concentrated

13   The long creamy whiteness of your tail

      pushes my love up above anything I can imagine
      I lose all features I can only feel
      the enchanting symptoms of your small, specific forepaws

      As these flood the moat of my heart with gratitude
      I recollect your great hind feet dangling off the ground
      beneath the even bigger power of your thighs

      lifted by your all-encompassing tail

      If I swoon I swoon to be the earth for you
      These are the days you walk the earth
      as whatever's up there will corroborate

      once my breath comes back

14

It's not rocket science
You either ride straight on
from the beginning
or you work back
over the whole thing

So why can't I tell
if I'm getting on
or off?

I'll ride that line into place
if the last thing I do is
the first thing I remember

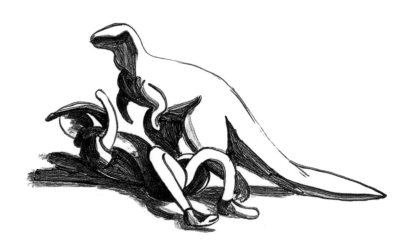

15

The door's open I'm
closed up in that
dream I can't watch
my eyes can't
shut that tight

Don't just stand there stupid
like a molasses factory in an earthquake
fuck me I can't watch

It's time to crush down on
the scared one
in the door
too late to shut

See all open
for whatever
you're too close
I can't watch

16   Some strong light
      shining from behind
      will show me the names
      if I don't fall off

      There's a dark divider
      between eyes and mind
      My back must know its name already
      No face when I turn around

      Come dark I'll turn around
      and remember the names
      facing from the great stage
      if I don't fall off

17

She girl sprawl doll
back thrown target shadow
still things can't move
moving blank want between

Leg up over marauding
toy sex hard play
tumbling rolling around flat
helpless fun falling helpless

Lifting head can't know
caught thrust instant only
get this never this
seeing can't see in

Long thick visible outside
pushy spell so obvious
dark half heart heading
down one way street

18   My perfect life soiled
     by this radioactive army food
     underfoot

     My beautiful sky
     don't touch it
     Now it's cloudy

     Oily data flowing
     and the river's dry
     True North's
     over

19　　Yes I admit it
I wandered around without it
not even knowing it
existed outside wanting something that must have been it
and not being there because not having it

Without that I can't be riding it
around agreeing that I do want it
and am around it
wanting it

20　　My experience has gotten a little away from me
Like I wake up and it's not today
So that's one problem

7 o'clock I'm not here then who is
That's another one

These are my days
and something's in the way
which makes three

Which means nothing
else matters
for the next little while

21   chaos imagines colossal strides

                                              x marks xmas upsidedown
          dogooding offshoot alcohol home

                                        memory scar me smooth
              nightshade kiss that's goodbye

                              no more next things
                  monumental horizon shoes kaput
                      shout shh walls hear
                    rage splashed dismal animal
                blister under clean clothes

                          dressed furniture falls sideways
              bedrock brain bedroom door

                              rug vacuum the stain
        a sort of dance

                                          counting up endless stairs

        fighting loss mess hop

22   That it will never come again
is what makes life so sweet
Before's no better off than never
My feet are in the sky

Believing what we don't believe
makes things happen twice
with nobody there the first time

There is no other time or place
or way here
except jump
Jump

23   Take that, That
And try some of this, This
Be yourself, Be
And don't tread on me, Don't

Fuck you, You
And I love it when you call me that, Love
Pleasure always goes twice around the block, Please
So say it again, Sam

One more time, Time
And another thing, Thing
Don't stop now, Now
Or else I'm gone, I

24 When we could move it was quick playing bodies
while the walls pretended to stand guard
we'd pin some things up, others we'd unhook
we believed the close smells, evenings led to afternoons

out from under he she it wrestling
with the built-in blanks it turned out
they made good enough blankets
to hold just about any amount of dust

and there was yeast
for unpredictability we'd
touch the continuity
and not get stuck

it was warm
booked in
bed, once
again

25   I toy with you
like I toy with my dick
I take it
and throw it

far away but find myself
somewhere strange, all the more
attached, a faithful acolyte worshiping
at your shrine, don't tell me
where, I want to guess

I wish you liked me more
Maybe when everything's all over

Like, like
like a cub waiting for the mother tongue all over
trembling like a still-life, don't tell me
who, I want to guess

26   Let the backlog be as long as it wants I don't care
let it dictate its history with furious accuracy
because I only want
to be on top
now

Your smooth mindless endless underside
is too continuous to exist
anywhere but
underneath

You don't have any parts and I
only have one thing I want
to be on top of you
Give me a kiss
you ass

27   Before you were you
      I was my own size

      Now that you're huge
      I'll still make you fit

28 Already you don't follow
    and how can you
    second guesses first thoughts smushed together

    Your tangled blank right where
    I'm trying to bend the line
    so you can see where
    it's going, but
    I've lost you haven't I?

    I appeal to the senses, ours
    Stars? That's Venus on the water
    both up and down
    the door lit
    if we weren't in our way

29 The last part to fall off
is the name clanging down
on the clown pile

Too bad say the seconds
That's nothing say the firsts

The light backs out
of its signatures
Cry your eyes out

I was the world's portal
judicious with my dowry
as a pine bough with its snow

Too bad, was
So sad, I

Carry them away
and drop them sideways in the snow

30   Just sitting here on a chair
     typing to write this
     the air circling
     and the day changing places
     with what comes next

     is
     the longer I think, quite a stretch

31

Isn't it a relief
to look at yourself
like you're somebody you
know to some extent

A kind of open-ended finitude to explore
behind the wrong shapes, clumsy habits
pleasure spots, hairy patches
matted names, wounds when you
get right down to it

In the dawn's early light, it was
"I see London, I see France"
but now, hoofing along underneath
what a relief

32   When you said
      "Astonish me"
      I didn't know what to do
      but I did think I knew
      what you meant

      But you just wanted to see
      me jump
      so you
      could smell inside

      Well I guess it's the same
      old unmentionable
      Pretty astonishing I bet

      I think I'll ride around on you
      and we'll see how astonishing that is

33   One two three, two two three
      One two three, two two three

      I'll sing you the tune of
      a genre I know

      It goes when you know two three
      I'm touching you two three

      That much we know two three
      No? two three? You two three

      You're holding me and we
      call this activity
      willed accidentally
      for all the world to see
      the genre of poetry

34

You'd think
a knowing hand, accurate body
sun on a
white wall
one glint
the way a mouth moved

You'd think a
good meal
nice smell
the right touches

Some little thing you'd think might
keep me
from pulling us down

35 Given any moment
thick as a book
transparent pages crowded with the supplest codes
open to beginner's eye and ear
tongue works too
unobtrusive replenishing instant
unfolding without pause

And say the whole was friendly
to each part
puppy, recorder, Camaro
each the perfect interpreter

Then say
we didn't want to read

36   No joints, no character

Rushing to please every breeze

Shoveled out of the present like Stupid here

Now it's me

Courtyard you won't leave as anything but a pile of sticks

37   So, poetry, I see you
swooned into steep trance

When I hear
your thin whisper
my arms are too light
I need your tail to write

It looks like I'm saying this to you
tranced in one oblique line
but your ear is everywhere
without it I'm all over the place

Really, I'm only
using you to write
what you tell me I hear

38	You laid siege
and now I
trample your plan

The vine grew
in your desire
but the vintage

is mine, my
words wet
with it I

taste the vantage
pouring your
hopes over you
from my sky

39 Outside any pyramid, life goes on
a big archaic mess tottering ahead
on its spindly nows and thens
nexts and spots of time sparkling
on the ocean flows of amnesia

Inside the head, something with a name
stays put, experience wrapping
an ever thicker hieroglyph around it
an empty circle underneath

Go figure, Zero!

40 I can't tell exactly
    where it's touching me
    I flew apart
    when it touched me there

    Anyway we're flying
    out of sight

    Look
    Right there
    An engine feet arms tail
    I can't tell

41

Pity me I'm screwed
around you I
won't stop holding
there's nothing else

It's
mine too
it's yours to give
Look at me

I don't care
if I've got it
backwards and you
always look away

There's nothing after
the last thing
I'll never stop
You have to

42   Heart I mind
you once above me
transparent stripping us
until we reached down

You pawed my chest
I see us
having it

Covered baskets were floating outside
hefts were gamboling
weaving

Arms paws chests careless
having happened
it keeps darting
Darling

43　The eye the mighty
the strong silent type

Ever hear of a mouth, full of
words one after another all sticking together?

We're not gliding above some
smooth "surface" all dotted with "things"

You think you're up there all alone
you and your tightlipped twin

Go on sleep tight
no time till you deign to wake
eternity under your thumb

We know you hear us out here

44   It's
a little long
stretching all afternoon

I know
it's sore with nothing
stretching out in front of you all the way

It's so big
but as long as I keep
my hand on you it'll stay away

45   Where the shutter fell
eye and memory still meet
locked out, penultimate, staring
for all the good that does

The only thing I remember
is you didn't have to look like anything else

But now that you do
memory stands guard
curled up

Rock-a-bye echo
good night sight
now the same
looks the same

46   Carry me to my own store
     I left my hole
     out in the rain all night

     Swing everything off the ground
     to the front just this once

     Only carry me
     No one else

     I'll tell you everything you want
     and whatever else
     It's okay to walk in the sugar
     There's more

47   Sleep would be perfect enough
      There anything fits
      inside anything
      like spoons

      It's fake when you wake
      but still, to dig
      deep in the tub
      where nothing's different

      First you have to get over the lip

      Nothing's stopping you

48

I can have packed,
parked, gone through
inspection, flown and met
that day's local infinity

I can have touched
those I love and spoken
phrases to those
I'll never see again

Everyone knows how boring dreams are
And yes, the fulcrum only works when you're awake
But the guy in the blue denim baseball cap
was he right when he said, "Killing me
is a war crime"?

49   Is this   part of
         this is   where you
      touch always   feel it
         at least   so I
      double so   know I
         when I   have places
      touch where   I can
         you're being   feel what
      touched I   it is
         know it's   being one
      there and   of us
         this is   touching you

50

Behold stout Somebody-or-Other
on that mountain
above the scrolling sea's
gold and silver wares

He's getting ready to sacrifice
the future to the past
or has already

The view can't say

No definitive blow
has emerged yet
from the competing tons
of bricks standing
on the backs
of tons of bricks

Underneath can't see
holding up the entire view

51   It may not look like much
but anyway, you're not supposed to look

Some things for family
lots for friends
some for old ones
some for new ones
for you, as much as you want

No reason to show more

52 Can it be said
I experience language as
an untranslatable vision of
my mother's face before
I knew the shapes
of words would come
back, over again in
thick endless repeated changing
novelty, the same shapes
in different places, saying
all the differences I'll
ever be able to
find in life and
infinitely more of course
which I say now
confidently ignorant of that
more which gives me
less, always, loss, permanent
to which I bow
in longing, saying it

Francie Shaw

These paintings are all still lifes of three small figures, two bendable people and a plastic dinosaur. They are intimate relationships which can be viewed as between two figures or different parts of oneself. At the same time they are clearly toys. As a whole the 52 paintings do not form any narrative progression; instead each poses variations of some basic question: is this play or struggle or both at once? What is the difference between terror and excitement, pleasure and pain? Who is carrying whom, who is in control?

Bob Perelman

One of my greatest pleasures is hearing Francie talk about paintings. In response to my first attempts to write a companion poem, she talked about the one that is now #3, telling me that I was just taking the point of view of one of the figures, but that for her both figures formed a single event. That put into words what I then recognized I had already been seeing in the paintings: passionate, hard-won instability, lability.

Dino, Guy-Puppet, Girl-Puppet–ersatz nature and historically real enough gender–the three figures are posed into an alphabet of primal postures. Spelling what? Eroticism pushing outward and intensifying or just little toy pictures? Subjectivity frames reason in these paintings. At the same time they stage flexible tragicomedies of the unnamable mixes of drive and reaction that course through our moments.

To try to meet this in words has been as exhilarating as those dreams where you can fly and as sobering as waking up.